Why Manners Matter

At School

Jillian Powell

W

FRANKLIN WATTS
LONDON · SYDNEY

First published in 2005 by
Franklin Watts
96 Leonard Street
London
EC2A 4XD

Franklin Watts Australia
45-51 Huntley Street
Alexandria, NSW 2015

Editor: Rachel Tonkin
Series design: Mo Choy
Art director: Jonathan Hair
Photography: Chris Fairclough
PSHE consultant: Wendy Anthony

With thanks to Years 4, 5 and 6
of Streatham Wells Primary School

A CIP catalogue record for this book is
available from the British Library

Dewey classification: 395.5

ISBN: 0 7496 6051 1

Printed in China

Contents

Going to school

Schools are busy places.
You learn, play and make
friends there, along with lots
of other children.

If you are kind to each other, you can make school a safer and nicer place for everyone.

?

What makes you happy or sad in the school playground?

Hello and goodbye

It is friendly to say hello when you see someone each day. It shows that you like them and care about their feelings.

When your mum, dad or a friend's parent takes you to school, you should remember to say goodbye and thank you.

Please and thank you

When you ask for something in class, remember to be polite and say please.

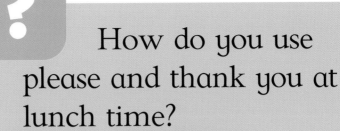

How do you use please and thank you at lunch time?

When someone helps you or gives you something, always say thank you.

Sharing

Sometimes you have to share things like books or computers. You help each other learn and it can be fun if you don't argue.

It's nice to help friends by lending them something they need.

Taking turns

Sometimes you need to be patient and wait for your turn when you are playing together.

What would happen if everyone tried to push to the front?

When you have to wait in a queue, it's not fair to try and push in front of others.

Teamwork

If you can work together as
a team, you will get more done.
It's more fun, too.

? How do you feel when others don't let you join in a game?

Playing together is a kind of teamwork, too. Be friendly and ask others to join in so that they don't feel left out.

15

Speaking and listening

When others are talking, you should listen and wait for your turn to speak. Then everyone can hear what is being said.

Listen carefully

You learn by listening, so don't chat in class when the teacher is speaking. If you are noisy, it stops others learning, too.

Telling the truth

You should tell the truth if you have done something wrong. It's not fair to let others take the blame.

THE ANCIENT GREEKS THOUGHT THEIR GODS LIVED TOGETHER ON TOP OF MOUNT OLYMPUS.

You should tell someone if
you think a friend is in trouble
or needs help.

Show you care

You can show a friend that you care by helping them when they are hurt or in trouble.

What would you do if you found a friend crying?

Do you remember your first day
at school? It helps to be nice
to new pupils and make them
feel welcome.

Think about . . .

Why it is important to care about other people's feelings . . .

? What should you do if you see a friend is upset?

? How does it help to listen to your friends?

? How do you feel if someone is nasty to you at school?

? What do you do if your friend is being bullied?

? How do you feel if you are nice to someone who is upset?

Think about why manners matter when
you are sharing things like books . . .

? What do you
say if a friend asks
to share your book?

? How do
you feel if a friend
won't let you share
a book?

? How could
sharing a book help
you learn and
have fun?

? If you don't
share with others, will
they share with you?

Index